DANGEROUS DRUGS

ECSTASY

CHRISTINE PETERSEN

Cavendish
Square

New York

Published in 2014 by Cavendish Square Publishing, LLC
303 Park Avenue South, Suite 1247, New York, NY 10010

Copyright © 2014 by Cavendish Square Publishing, LLC

First Edition

CPSIA Compliance Information: Batch #WW14CSQ

All websites were available and accurate when this book was sent to press.

Library of Congress Cataloging-in-Publication Data
Petersen, Christine.
Ecstasy / by Christine Petersen.
p. cm. — (Dangerous drugs)
Includes index.
ISBN 978-1-62712-375-4 (hardcover) ISBN 978-1-62712-376-1(paperback)
ISBN 978-1-62712-377-8 (ebook)
1. Ecstasy (Drug) — Juvenile literature. 2. Drug abuse — Juvenile literature. I. Petersen, Christine. II. Title.
RM666.M35 P48 2014
615.7883—dc23

EDITORIAL DIRECTOR: Dean Miller
SENIOR EDITOR: Peter Mavrikis
SERIES DESIGNER: Kristen Branch

Photo research by Kristen Branch

The photographs in this book are used by permission and through the courtesy of: Cover photo by © SuperStock; © SuperStock, 1; Exactostock/Superstock, 4; © mediacolor's/Alamy, 8; © FDA/Alamy, 10; © Angela Hampton Picture Library/Alamy, 12; David Hoffman Photo Library/Alamy, 15; © BSIP SA/Alamy, 18; fStop Images/the Agency Collection/Getty Images, 22; ©Everynight Images/Alamy, 26; Image Source/Superstock, 29; Michelle Del Guercio/Photo Researchers/Getty Images, 32; © Jake Lyell/Alamy, 33; © AF archive/Alamy, 35; BSIP/Superstock, 40; Steve Debenport/E+/Getty Images, 42; © iStock.com/Simmisimons, 43; © Danita Delimont/Alamy, 45; Noel Hendrickson/Blend Images/Getty Images, 46; ©iStockphoto.com/DenGuy, 48; © Golden Pixels LLC/Alamy, 50; MIXA/Getty Images, 52; SW productions/Photodisc/Getty Images, 54.

Printed in the United States of America

Contents

CHAPTER ONE

Hidden Dangers

HAVE YOU EVER EXPERIENCED A MOMENT of happiness so perfect that it filled your heart? Perhaps that feeling struck you after meeting a special person or achieving a long sought-after goal. Then again, it might have bubbled up at the most ordinary of moments: while laughing with family at the dinner table, hanging out with friends, or taking a walk in the park. This joyful emotion is also known as **ecstasy**.

Left: When used to describe an emotion, the word "ecstasy" is often associated with a strong feeling of joy or delight.

Humans want to feel happy, especially in the company of other people. But like all emotions, ecstasy happens only when the circumstances are perfect. It can't be planned or faked. Perhaps that's why **drugs** like MDMA (methylenedioxymethamphetamine) have become so popular. MDMA creates feelings that mimic **euphoria** (joy) or **empathy** (understanding of others' feelings). That's how this drug earned its nickname: Ecstasy. But MDMA does not only affect mood. It can make shy people feel self-confident, or provide a burst of energy that lasts for several hours. MDMA also enhances the senses by making lights, sounds, and touch more intense. Those tempting side effects make Ecstasy sound harmless. But the truth is far more complicated.

History of The Hug Drug

In 1912, scientists at Merck Pharmaceuticals were working overtime. Their competitor, Bayer, had a product that could control abnormal bleeding. Merck wanted to develop a similar drug that would be less expensive. **Synthesis** (manufacturing) of this drug required several steps. MDMA was produced during one stage of the synthesis. At the time, MDMA wasn't considered a drug (a substance that

changes how the body or brain functions). Instead, it was tucked away on a shelf among other unused chemicals and all but forgotten.

The real story of MDMA begins in 1965. That year, chemist Alexander Shulgin synthesized MDMA while working for Dow Chemical Company. A few years later, he heard that people were taking it as a drug. Shulgin was curious about its mind-altering effects. He tried MDMA with his wife, Ann. In turn, Ann began giving the drug to patients she treated in therapy. She believed that it helped them to relax and let go of their fear and anger. Within a few years, dozens of therapists nationwide had begun to use the drug in treatment.

By the early 1980s, MDMA had spread from chemistry labs and therapy offices to dance clubs and **raves**. Young people called it Ecstasy, and deejays created a whole new style of music to play while dancers "rolled" under its influence. Before long, college students were familiar with this drug, too. They knew what to expect as it took effect. A restless feeling was common, along with sweatiness and a dry mouth. Users might notice an increased heart rate, as if they had just been startled. People would sometimes grind their teeth or clench their jaws

Ecstasy is a potent drug that first became popular in nightclubs, raves, and dance parties. Known as a "club drug," many users believe that Ecstasy enhances their nightlife experience with feelings of increased alertness and a strong sense of well-being.

tightly. Others experienced chills, nausea, or headaches.

Users were strangely willing to endure these symptoms along with Ecstasy's more desirable side effects. But health professionals were concerned. As the drug became more widespread, so were its **adverse reactions**. Hospitals admitted people who became ill after a single dose. They saw others who collapsed despite previously using the drug without problems. These patients suffered a frightening range of symptoms, such as

severe dehydration, high body temperatures, and swelling of the brain. Some experienced seizures or kidney failure, and a few fell into comas. Medical researchers began to study the effects of MDMA on animals. They found that the drug damages nerve cells in the brain, perhaps permanently.

Meanwhile, law enforcement officials noticed an increase in the **trafficking** (illegal sales) of Ecstasy. Drug sales between the United States and other countries were on the rise. The US Drug Enforcement Agency (DEA) decided it was time to take action. Up to this point, MDMA had been legal. But in 1985, the DEA used a law called the Controlled Substances Act to ban the drug. It was now a felony to use, buy, or produce MDMA in the United States.

Monitoring Ecstasy

Since 1975, researchers at the University of Michigan have conducted a study called *Monitoring the Future* (MTF). Almost 50,000 teens nationwide take this confidential survey each year. They answer questions about personal drug use, and share their attitudes about specific drugs. Ecstasy was added to MTF's middle- and high-school

9

THE DRUG SCHEDULE

The Controlled Substances Act was passed in 1970. Under this federal law, the DEA evaluates drugs to compare their risks and benefits. Each drug is categorized into one of five drug schedules, or categories.

In 1985, Ecstasy was placed on Schedule I along with lysergic acid diethylamide (LSD), heroin, and other **recreational drugs**. Substances in this category have no proven use in medicine. Instead, they are used for personal enjoyment. Many recreational drugs are addictive or can cause serious health problems. By placing Ecstasy on Schedule I, the DEA made its use illegal. It is a felony to have Ecstasy tablets in your possession. Those who sell, buy, or manufacture this drug face heavier penalties. This may include a sentence of several years in prison and thousands of dollars in fines.

Medicinal drugs are used to treat or prevent diseases. Yet some are still abused like recreational drugs. Schedule II is a list of medicines with the greatest risk of abuse. These include OxyContin, Ritalin, cocaine, and methamphetamine (also known as crystal meth). Health care professionals must prescribe these drugs carefully and track their use. Schedules III, IV, and V contain drugs such as Vicodin, Xanax, and Lomotil. These have lesser risk factors and are still monitored. It is a felony to use or possess a drug on any of these schedules without a legal doctor's prescription written especially for you.

Ecstasy is often taken orally and is usually distributed as a small pill.

questionnaires in 1996. The results were gloomy. Although this drug was relatively new, its use was already widespread. Almost as many eighth graders (2.3 percent) as college students (2.8 percent) were using Ecstasy. Worse, the survey showed that 4.6 percent of tenth and twelfth graders had tried it at least once.

Would you be surprised to learn that almost as many middle- and high-school students used Ecstasy in 2010 as in 1996? Several factors influence teen drug use:

- Level of awareness of a drug's particular risks
- Social disapproval
- Access to the drug

According to MTF, in 2011, only 25.4 percent of eighth graders believed there was "great risk" in using Ecstasy once or twice. Adding to this problem, social

12

disapproval of Ecstasy is low compared to previous years. In other words, kids don't think badly of each other for taking this drug once or twice. They may even consider it cool. The only good news concerns access. MTF data suggest that it has become slightly more difficult for teens to obtain Ecstasy.

Impure

If you have strep throat, the doctor may prescribe an antibiotic. You'll go to a pharmacy to obtain that medicine. The Food and Drug Administration (FDA) oversees the manufacturing of antibiotics and other medicinal drugs in the United States. This agency requires that medicines are pure and carefully labeled. Each pill in your antibiotic bottle will contain exactly the same dose of medicine and no other ingredients. Pharmaceutical companies are careful to uphold health and safety standards. They may lose customers or be put out of business if products don't meet FDA standards.

Schedule I drugs, such as Ecstasy, are not monitored to ensure their safety or quality. Ecstasy can be manufactured almost anywhere—in a high-tech lab or someone's dingy garage. This lack of supervision creates serious risks.

The first relates to dosage, which can vary wildly from tablet to tablet. One pill may contain as little as 50 milligrams of MDMA. Another, which looks identical in every way, could hold as much as 300 mg. Effects from low doses of Ecstasy last three to six hours. As you might guess, a higher-dose pill will intensify those effects and make them last longer. The higher dose also significantly increases the risk of adverse reactions.

Ecstasy users must also worry about the steadily increasing problem of **adulteration**. Illegal drug labs are not concerned about your safety. These labs make drugs for profit and save money wherever possible. One solution is to replace MDMA with fillers and cheaper drugs. Ecstasy tablets collected during drug raids are often tested. These have been found to contain everything from talcum powder and caffeine to dangerous drugs that include amphetamine and methamphetamine.

Ecstasy manufacturers work hard to distract you from the risks. MDMA is manufactured in powder form. In labs, colorful dyes are added. The resulting paste is pressed into individual tablets. These are stamped with cutesy symbols such as cartoon characters or familiar product logos. You might mistake these pills for candy. They certainly

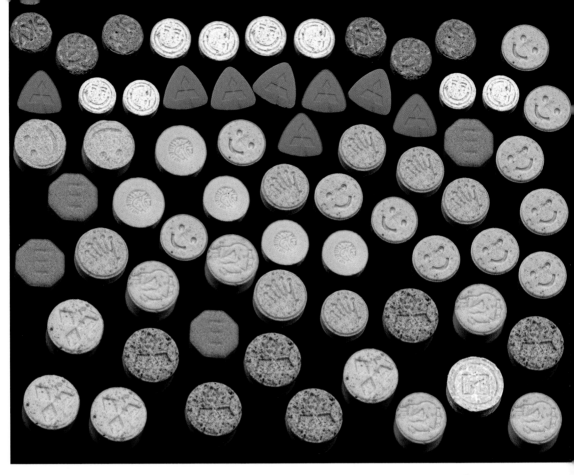

Dosages of MDMA often vary from pill to pill. Illegal drug labs do not worry about safety when manufacturing Ecstasy. This may lead to dangerous—and potentially deadly—results.

don't look dangerous. Have you heard the biblical parable about the wolf in sheep's clothing? A wolf disguises itself in sheepskin. It sneaks onto the pasture to graze among the flock. Because the wolf looks familiar, the sheep ignores it—until the wolf attacks. Ecstasy has a lot in common with that tricky wolf. It may look harmless, but a multitude of dangers are hidden within.

CHAPTER TWO

The Chemical Connection

NO ONE REALLY KNOWS WHY CERTAIN experiences make us feel joyful. But neuroscientists, who study the nervous system, are beginning to understand *how* the brain reacts when a person is happy.

The central nervous system includes millions of nerve cells in the brain and spinal cord. Nerve cells respond to input from all of your senses. They react when you are injured. If you need to run, they fire into action. The same is true when you experience emotions. This system works because nerve cells can send messages. Have you ever played the game Telephone? Several people stand in a line. The first person whispers something to the second, and the message is continued down the line. Telephone

can be a funny game, because people often forget parts of the story or mishear the message. But the nervous system is usually very accurate.

Nerve cells are designed to conduct signals. Each cell is tipped with two kinds of long, finger-like branches. At one end are tufts of dendrites that bring messages into the cell. The opposite end of a nerve cell bears an arm-like axon. Reaching toward the next cell, it passes the message along. Signals move through nerve cells in the form of electricity. But electricity cannot flow across a **synapse**, the small, liquid space between cells. Instead, the pulse of electricity causes the axon to release chemicals called **neurotransmitters**.

Like microscopic rafts, neurotransmitters float across the synapse. They attach to **receptors** on nearby dendrites. Receptors are like locks, and neurotransmitters are the keys: they cannot dock unless the fit is perfect. When the connection is made, an electrical signal begins to flow. In this way, the message is passed through many nerve cells to its final destination.

Special "trash collector" molecules pick up neuro-transmitters from their docks. Most neurotransmitters are returned to their original axons. This recycling sys-

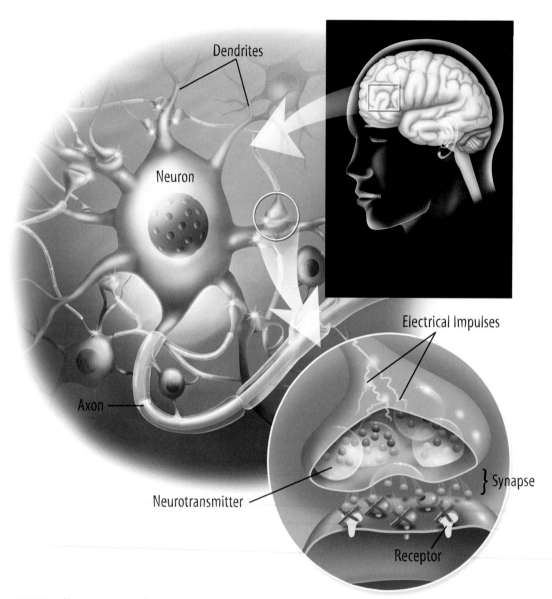

Dendrites

Neuron

Axon

Electrical Impulses

Neurotransmitter

} Synapse

Receptor

MDMA affects activity of the brain's chemical messengers known as neurotransmitters. These changes result in a wide variety of symptoms, including a rapid heart rate and jitteriness.

tem guarantees that your nervous system is always ready for action. All this is crucial because nerve signals control almost everything we do and feel.

Your Brain on Ecstasy

More than 100 different neurotransmitters have been found in humans. Only three of these cause most of the "symptoms" we associate with joy: a faster heart rate, tingling skin, increased alertness, and a sense of well-being. The drug Ecstasy scrambles the normal flow of those same three neurotransmitters. And it has an especially strong influence on **serotonin**. This transmitter controls the intensity of your responses. It also affects a wide range of bodily processes and behaviors, from mood and alertness to digestion. Serotonin even plays a role in visual perception, changing how your brain interprets what you see.

Ecstasy is absorbed through the digestive system. The drug is then carried through the bloodstream to the nervous system. Here is where the problems begin. Remember those "trash collector" molecules that usually recycle serotonin? When MDMA is present, these molecules collect the drug instead of serotonin. Imagine trying to fit more people into an already overcrowded room.

As MDMA begins to enter nerve cells, all the stored serotonin is forced out. Serotonin rapidly builds up in synapses throughout your brain and spinal cord, affecting many of the body's systems. That's why Ecstasy users experience such a wide range of symptoms, from rapid heart rate and jitteriness to nausea and sweating.

You may be getting the picture that Ecstasy takes over your nervous system like pirates capture an unwary ship. Realize that there's a price for turning over the wheel to this chemical pirate. MDMA "steals" your body's serotonin by causing it to be "used up" all at once. It can take up to two weeks for serotonin levels to recover. You'll feel a hangover because your body has lost the serotonin that would normally regulate certain body systems. Common symptoms include exhaustion, grouchiness, sadness, poor memory, and restless sleep.

The hangover is merely the tip of the iceberg. When Ecstasy highjacks your serotonin levels, the results can be deadly.

Too Hot

In the United States, the Drug Abuse Warning Network (DAWN) reports on drug-related hospitalizations. Almost

1.2 million Americans were hospitalized in 2010 after taking recreational drugs. About 22,000 of these cases involved Ecstasy. That number has more than doubled since 2004. Take note of this fact: 72 percent of those harmed by Ecstasy were between the ages of 12 and 24.

Ecstasy **overdose** can occur anywhere the drug is used—at house parties and after-school hangouts, or even in your own room. But raves attract crowds that increase the risk. In May 2010, 16,000 techno music fans gathered at a rave held in a San Francisco-area sports arena. Ravers were told that undercover police officers would be in the crowed. Warnings were posted that people selling, carrying, or using drugs would be arrested. As the music began, ravers poured onto the arena floor and began to dance. Some were as young as sixteen. Police officers made seventy-three arrests. They also helped paramedics assist people who fell ill.

Among many other roles, serotonin helps to regulate body temperature. As this neurotransmitter floods the nervous system during Ecstasy use, the body's temperature may skyrocket. This condition is called **hyperthermia**. Hours of dancing in a crowded, poorly ventilated setting can increase this effect. Serotonin also blocks unpleasant

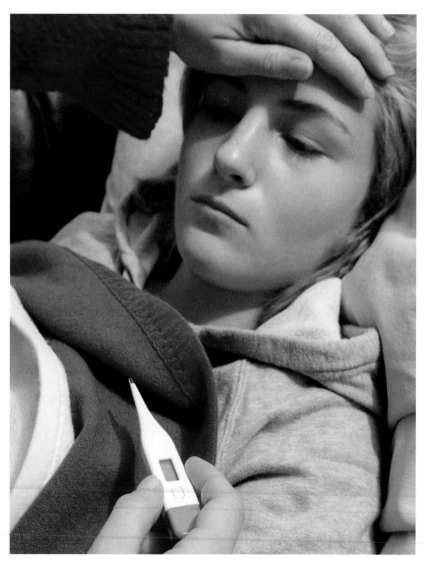

MDMA can cause hyperthermia. Flooded with seratonin, the body fails to regulate its own temperature or to recognize the heat caused by excessive physical activity and poor ventilation.

feelings. An Ecstasy user may not realize that their temperature is so high. They may continue dancing until severe symptoms strike.

Symptoms of hyperthermia include nausea, headaches, and low blood pressure, which cause dizziness. Without treatment, hyperthermia can lead to seizures, organ failure, and possibly death. That's exactly what happened at the rave in San Francisco. Eight people were hospitalized for severe Ecstasy overdose. Some experienced body temperatures as high as 107°F (41.7°C) before they could be stabilized. Two other young people, with symptoms too extreme to treat, died.

Drowning

The body may lose as much as a half-gallon (2 liters) of sweat for every hour of energetic exercise. Sweat cools you down by moving water from cells inside the body to the surface of the skin.

After so much exercise, a person naturally feels thirsty. Ecstasy increases the urge to drink water. It may even prevent the user from realizing when to stop drinking. The drug sometimes also blocks the body's signal to begin sweating. The result is an imbalance between water and sodium in the cells. The body uses this salt to conduct electrical signals through the nervous system. Sodium is also important to maintain blood pressure. When there is more water than salt outside cells, water rushes into cells to establish balance. It is as if they are being flooded or drowned. Physicians refer to this condition as **hyponatremia**.

Hyponatremia causes cells throughout the body to swell. The patient experiences painful symptoms including muscle cramps, nausea, and vomiting, and sometimes convulsions. What happens in the brain? Here, cells are confined within the solid "helmet" of the skull. There's no room for cells to expand. The result is confusion, headache, **hallucinations**, or coma. If treatment cannot be provided in time, hyponatremia causes death.

Just one month after the deaths of two ravers in San Francisco, another arena-based rave was held in Los Angeles. This event attracted approximately 185,000 people. About 120 were treated in emergency rooms for overdose and other drug-related health complaints. A 15-year-old girl was admitted to the rave despite its advertised age limit. She began to experience hyperthermia after taking a dose of Ecstasy. As her temperature rose,

the teen began drinking large amounts of water. She eventually collapsed and was trampled under the feet of the packed crowd. The girl was taken to a local hospital and later died of hyponatremia.

Some young people never attend a rave, but they may still be at risk of hyponatremia. Have you ever seen friends drink alcohol at a house party or after-school hangout? Mixing alcohol with Ecstasy is especially risky. In part, that's because alcohol is a depressant drug. It slows down the body, so it seems to reduce Ecstasy's stimulating effects. A user may take more Ecstasy, thinking their first dose was too small. Like Ecstasy, alcohol dehydrates the body. Put the two together and you have a recipe for hyponatremia.

Too Much Prevention

Many young people have heard that Ecstasy can cause dehydration. They drink large amounts of water after using the drug, thinking this will allow them to safely dance all night. A British case reveals the dangers of this "preventive medicine."

In 2002, a 20-year-old British woman went to a rave. She and several friends took Ecstasy and then began to drink water. The woman

was not a first-time Ecstasy user and had apparently tried this trick before. This time, however, she began to feel ill. Her friends had heard it was helpful to rest. They suggested she lay down in a quiet room. A few hours later, the young woman experienced a massive seizure. Despite receiving treatment in an emergency room, she later died from hyponatremia. Doctors evaluated her body weight, blood tests, and the amount of swelling. They calculated that this young woman must have consumed approximately 2.6 gallons (10 L) of water in a nine-hour period after taking one dose of Ecstasy.

Data from this case shed some light on the risk factors for hyponatremia. Women may be more likely to suffer this condition than men. That's because the same dose of Ecstasy may have a larger effect on women's smaller bodies. Youths may also be at greater risk. They have proportionately more healthy brain cells to swell in a hyponatremia attack than do older people.

CHAPTER THREE

The Agony of Ecstasy

IN 2001, RESEARCHERS AT WASHINGTON University School of Medicine conducted a study of active Ecstasy users. The data provided some important but troubling insights. For example, 63 percent of all participants admitted that they continued to use Ecstasy "despite knowledge of physical or psychological problems from it." In other words, many young people actually understand that Ecstasy is not "risk-free." They ignore this fact in favor of the drug's potential pleasurable side effects.

Hopefully, you know better. You've already learned that a single dose of Ecstasy can lead to life-threatening health reactions. Some users get lucky and never encounter

Many users mistakenly believe that Ecstasy is not an addictive drug, and continue to take it despite the serious affects that it may have to their health.

these problems, but that doesn't mean they've escaped the dangers of Ecstasy. The first of these is **tolerance**. This occurs when the nervous system adjusts to the drug. The Washington University study revealed that tolerance develops among many users. Thirty-five percent of study participants noticed that their usual dose became less effective. To overcome tolerance and get the same "high" sensations, a user may choose to take a larger dose.

Users will likely never experience the same, supposedly blissful sensations they got from a first dose of Ecstasy.

But that doesn't stop people from trying. Ecstasy users may turn to dangerous methods to overcome tolerance. Among these are "stacking" and "piggybacking." Stacking involves taking several pills at once. A user piggybacks by popping a second pill as the first is wearing off. Other users turn to far riskier habits. They may snort MDMA in powder form or inject it in a liquid.

Any of these methods may lead to **dependence**. Drug dependence occurs when a user does not feel normal unless he or she can take the drug regularly. The user may feel physically tired and bad-tempered without the drug. He or she may have trouble sleeping, concentrating, or remembering things. Depression can be a very serious side effect of Ecstasy dependence. Forty-three percent of Ecstasy users in the Washington University study qualified as dependent.

The Drug Abuse Warning Network collects data on people who are hospitalized for dependence as well as drug reactions. In 2009, more than 1,000 Americans visited emergency rooms (ER) because of Ecstasy dependence. They needed medical help to break away from this drug. That number may seem small, but notice the trend: In the short period from 2006 to 2009, the number of ER admissions for Ecstasy **withdrawal** more than doubled.

30

Not What You Bargained For

Law enforcement officials are concerned with the dramatic increase of Ecstasy trafficking between Canada and the United States. Between 2005 and 2006, the amount of Ecstasy seized on the US-Canadian border increased tenfold. Drug trafficking makes more Ecstasy available in the United States. Worse, this flow of drugs increases the risk of impure Ecstasy. Fifty-five percent of Ecstasy seized on the US-Canadian border in 2006 contained methamphetamine.

Ecstasy has long been known as the "hug drug" because MDMA makes users friendly and touchy. But that reputation is changing. Methamphetamine is a **stimulant** drug. You may know it as "crystal meth." Like MDMA, it provides energy. But methamphetamine also makes users edgy. This drug lowers inhibitions, meaning that users are likely to take risks without thinking. They may be aggressive. Instead of hugging, kids on Ecstasy are now sometimes fighting. They are also more sexually active. That opens a whole new set of problems, including pregnancy, sexually transmitted diseases, and sexual assault. Methamphetamine is also highly addictive. Withdrawal from methamphetamine causes deep depression

31

and powerful cravings for the drug that can be difficult to overcome. The worst part is that users believe they are taking Ecstasy. They may have no idea they have been exposed to this other terrible drug.

During 2011 and 2012, at least twenty-seven people died and hundreds of others were hospitalized in

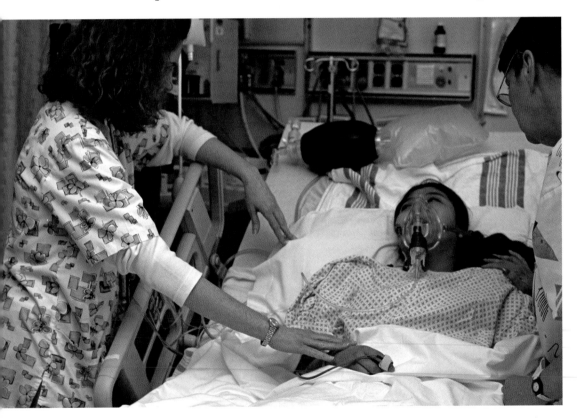

Symptoms of Ecstasy overdose include high blood pressure, seizures, hyperthermia, stroke, or organ failure. Unless one receives immediate medical attention, an overdose may lead to death.

the Canadian provinces of Alberta and British Columbia. They had taken Ecstasy laced with PMMA (paramethoxymethamphetamine). PMMA has effects similar to Ecstasy but acts more slowly. Regular Ecstasy users may notice this difference. Believing that they have gotten a low dose, they may take another pill. Once PMMA kicks in, however, it is even more dangerous than Ecstasy. A particular concern is PMMA's rapid ability to elevate body temperature. In early 2012, five young

Watch for early warning signs of Ecstasy overdose, such as headache, faintness, and vomiting.

Canadian men were arrested for possessing and selling Ecstasy laced with PMMA. The lab responsible for the manufacturing of the drug has not yet been located. The Calgary Police Service warned that more of the drug might still be in circulation and advised people not to use any form of Ecstasy.

The Gateway

Ecstasy is sometimes described as a **gateway drug**. People may try it as their first drug and feel that it's harmless, so they go on to try others. Users may become tolerant of Ecstasy and seek other drugs to replace its "high." Some people go through that "gateway" accidentally when they take adulterated Ecstasy not knowing that the drugs added can also be addictive. Users may seek those drugs out without even realizing they've been exposed. George Alan O'Dowd has firsthand experience of the Ecstasy gateway.

O'Dowd became famous in 1982 as Boy George, lead singer of '80s new-wave band Culture Club. At that moment, life should have been wonderful for Boy George. He had several chart-topping hits, fame, and money. But mostly, George felt overwhelmed. The press surrounded him. Record company officials demanded more hits. And it looked like his relationship was about to fall apart.

One night at a club, George was offered Ecstasy, which he decided to take. Within half an hour, he forgot all his worries. Everything seemed right in his world. George loved the feeling, and Ecstasy seemed so safe that he began trying other drugs. Soon he was using cocaine, and eventually switched to heroin. Years later, George could

Boy George, the lead singer of Culture Club, battled drug addiction for many years.

look back and see how Ecstasy served as a gateway drug for him. "One [drug] led to another," he wrote in his 1995 autobiography, "like steppingstones across a murky stream."

After sixteen years of sobriety, George thought he could handle using the drugs again. The decision to use again in 2005 landed him in prison. Now clean, he continues to

DON'T JOIN THIS CLUB

Ecstasy is often grouped with other mind-altering substances called "club drugs." As the name suggests, these drugs became popular in clubs and raves. But its use has spread to many other settings, especially in urban areas. Young people now routinely use Ecstasy and other club drugs at house parties. They take club drugs while hanging out after school and may even use them at home. Like Ecstasy, each of the club drugs can cause a variety of severe reactions. The threat is multiplied when drugs are mixed, which unfortunately, is a common practice.

Drug dealers and others may take advantage of young people who are high on Ecstasy, encouraging them to try these other drugs. Beware: many club drugs have intense and frightening effects. For example, GHB and Rohypnol have been called "date-rape drugs." Both can cause a form of amnesia, making the user susceptible to sexual assault. But because victims have no clear memory of the event, these cases can be difficult to prove or prosecute. Ketamine was developed as an **anesthetic** (painkilling drug) and was used during veterinary surgeries. It's fast acting and causes a dreamy sensation of numbness. Even at low doses, Ketamine can affect memory. At high doses, it produces frightening hallucinations.

DRUG	SOME ADVERSE REACTIONS
Ecstasy	Dehydration, dangerously increased body temperature, short- or long-term memory loss
GHB (gamma-hydroxybutyric acid)	Slowed heart rate and breathing, seizures, coma
Methamphetamine	Overexcitement, paranoia (unreasonable fear and suspicion), weight loss, heart or nervous system damage
Ketamine	Loss of coordination, inability to pay attention, depression, high blood pressure, fatal breathing difficulties
Rohypnol	Amnesia, decreased blood pressure, dizziness, confusion
LSD (lysergic acid diethylamide)	Increased body temperature, tremors, numbness, paranoia, "flashbacks"

create music while working on maintaining a healthy life-style. Boy George's story is one of thousands that prove drugs control the user, not the other way around.

A Lot to Lose

Ecstasy might appear to bring you closer to friends for a few hours. Or it may feel like a solution to your problems. But even if you only use it now and then, Ecstasy will impact your life. The hangover will leave you out of sorts for days afterward. You may argue more frequently with family members and feel irritated by the same friends you bonded with just days before. Meanwhile, your school-work will probably suffer. What about sports? It's hard to compete when you haven't eaten or slept well. Keep in mind that school sports teams can drop you for drug use. But there's more to lose than your spot on a team this year. Colleges look at your school record. They may deny scholar-ships or even refuse acceptance if you've been suspended from school or prosecuted in court on a drug offense.

Believe it or not, those may be the best outcomes. Ecstasy is a Schedule I drug, so it's a felony merely to be caught with it in your possession. Buying, selling, and manufacturing Ecstasy are yet more serious crimes. If arrested for any of

these offenses, you face serious time in detention or prison. That mistake may stay on your record for years to come, affecting, or even cancelling, many future opportunities.

You should also consider the long-term effects of Ecstasy on your body. Medical studies indicate that MDMA is a **neurotoxin**: it damages nerve endings. This harmful effect is especially noticeable in the brain's **cerebral cortex** and **hippocampus**. The cerebral cortex controls many essential functions of the "thinking" brain. It's in charge of memory, attention, reasoning, and planning. The hippocampus helps to store memories, so it is crucial to learning.

Professor Konstantine Zakzanis, from the University of Toronto, examined the long-term effects of Ecstasy on the brain. His first study included a mix of 24 current Ecstasy users and 24 people who had never used the drug. Dr. Zakzanis tested each person's ability to organize ideas logically, recall details of a story, and follow steps to solve problems. He found that the Ecstasy users scored lower on almost every part of the test. Next he observed a different group of fifteen active Ecstasy users. Over a period of a year, all showed declines in learning abilities and memory. Two years later, Dr. Zakzanis retested the same group

Ecstasy users can suffer from memory loss, including the inability to remember details of a story or recall visual patterns, including the shapes and colors used in a memory test.

of people. Seven were still using Ecstasy. Their scores were worse than they had been two years before. The other eight subjects had stopped using Ecstasy. This group showed no change in memory and learning ability, or scored slightly higher. The score was tied to a user's level of previous use. Heavier users were less likely to show improvement. Are you willing to take that chance?

CHAPTER FOUR

Starting and Stopping

YOUNG PEOPLE HAVE MANY REASONS for trying Ecstasy. Among these, three stand out:
- Kids want to feel closer to friends,
- they feel pressured by peers, and
- they are seeking an escape from life's problems.

Some people, though they may want to, find it difficult to show physical affection. There is an especially strong expectation for boys to keep a physical distance from each other. They may think that hugging other boys looks weak, or fear being called "gay." Yet studies show that boys are drawn to the effects of Ecstasy. According to the 2009 *Youth Risk Behavior Surveillance Survey* (YRBSS), teen boys were 38 percent more likely to try Ecstasy than girls. Data from the DAWN supports this observation. In 2009, 61 percent of young people admitted to hospitals for Ecstasy abuse were boys. Teen boys benefit if they can let down their guard with friends. But using Ecstasy is not a good solution. The "relaxing" effects of Ecstasy can encourage users toward risky behaviors,

Some teens believe that Ecstasy helps them "loosen up" through the feeling of euphoria and improved social connection.

from binge drinking to driving while high. It also places boys in that "gateway" leading to use of other drugs.

Peer pressure is a subtle force. The message is intense: "You must look and behave like others in order to have friends. If not, you will miss out on life's best experiences and opportunities." Most of the time, peers have only as much power as we give them. But that can be hard to see in the moment. This is especially true because our brains

Many teens feel uncomfortable using drugs but feel pressured to try them by friends and acquaintances.

learn primarily by imitation. When we see others act a certain way, it can be hard to resist doing the same thing. Teens face another hurdle: Portions of the brain that control reasoning and impulses don't fully develop until about the age of twenty-five. Yet even adults struggle to overcome peer pressure. The search for acceptance can lead to questionable or even dangerous choices.

Katherine Jenkins provides an example. Today, this young Welsh singer is known worldwide for her ability to perform opera and popular music with equal brilliance and flair. In her teens, however, Jenkins got involved with "a bad crowd." With them, she began using Ecstasy and other drugs. As she admits, "it just made me fit in better." It took a rare opportunity for Jenkins to choose to break away from the drugs: she was offered a recording contract. She knew she'd never succeed if she continued to use. Now Jenkins encourages young people to avoid that path completely. "I regret it massively," she has said.

In the worst cases, peer pressure escalates to bullying. Victims of bullying may be teased painfully or even physically assaulted by peers. Young people who are bullied may not know how to ask for help. They may even begin to feel as if they deserve the abuse. It's easy to

assume that adults won't understand what's happening. Kids in these difficult situations may simply want to hide and erase the pain. Ecstasy seems like a solution.

Peer pressure is not the only challenge for young people. Imagine being so poor that your parents can't provide enough to eat. What if your home is in a neighborhood where you don't feel safe to walk down the street? That's the reality for many young people living in urban

Despite the difficult challenges faced daily by many youths, no form of any drug should be considered a solution.

areas. But it is not only the poor who feel misery. At the opposite end of the spectrum, kids from middle-class and wealthy backgrounds may receive little attention from busy parents. Some of these young people experience unbearable pressure to succeed at school or in sports. In all these cases, teens may use Ecstasy to ease their stress.

Young people may begin to use drugs if they feel lonely or overstressed by family expectations.

Self-Check

If you're already using Ecstasy, take a moment to look honestly at your behavior. Can you identify with any of these statements?

- I have to take more Ecstasy to get the same effect I had during my first experience.
- I have begun to use the drug more often.
- I've started trying other drugs.
- I spend a lot of time thinking about Ecstasy: *How can I get more? When can I next use it?*
- I feel different since using the drug. I'm moody, have changed friends, am spending more time alone, or am less concerned with success at school or work.
- I don't feel well when I can't use Ecstasy.

These are some of the signs of Ecstasy dependence. If *any* fit you, it's time to ask for help. You might feel scared or alone. Even if it's difficult, find a trusted adult and share your story. Your parents are often your best support in difficult times. If you can't go to them, reach out to a trusted teacher, school counselor, or religious leader. Your

Teens experiencing issues with drugs can seek help by talking to a trained counselor or calling a support hotline.

doctor can also provide advice about overcoming drug dependence. Unless you are a danger to yourself or others, all information you share with a physician is private.

Drug hotlines are anonymous resources when all else fails. You'll find phone numbers and websites among the resources at the end of this book. You may find other online sites with forums and chat rooms. But remember: never share personal information over the Internet. People may not be who they seem.

48

LETTING GO

To recover from drug dependence, you must be dedicated, honest, and patient. You might seek out a Nar-Ateen or other teen-focused twelve-step meetings. These meetings are held in many cities and towns. Kids who attend these meetings see that they are not alone. They learn to support each other through the challenges of recovery.

Inpatient and outpatient treatment are also available. These are good choices if you need a more structured environment to stop using Ecstasy, alcohol, or other drugs. Inpatient treatment takes place in a hospital-like setting. You receive medical care as the drugs leave your system. Counselors talk with you about setting goals and avoiding drug temptations. Families often participate in these sessions so that you can learn to communicate and solve problems.

Outpatient treatment has similar goals, except that you live at home. Your treatment might involve a blend of private, family, and peer group counseling. Meanwhile, you can stay in school and pursue other daily activities. Drug treatment is not an easy process. But it helps you gain the skills and strength to build a future free of drugs.

Seeing the Signs

You are learning the dangers of this drug and may choose to avoid it. But your friends are probably still unaware. You can look out for them. A first step is to share your knowledge. You don't have to be pushy, just mention it in a casual way and see how the conversation plays out. Keep in mind that your friends may not make the choice to stop using. It's not helpful to nag them. If you care, you also can't look the other way. Look for signs of trouble and offer help if needed.

Here are some typical indicators of Ecstasy overdose. If you're with someone who exhibits two or more of these, call an adult immediately or dial 911.

Physical signs:
- Dilated eye pupils
- Rapid or irregular heart rate
- Shallow breathing
- Nausea or vomiting
- Tremors or seizures
- Fever

Mental signs:
- Extreme nervousness
- Paranoia
- Confusion

CHAPTER FIVE

The Power of Choice

DURING THE YEAR 1987, AMERICA'S TOP three television networks ran thousands of commercials. Viewers watched Michael Jackson sing and dance for Pepsi. They were amazed by IBM's newest personal computer. Phone companies advertised long-distance calling plans. Costumed creatures invited kids to eat fast-food meals. But it was a series of public service announcements (PSAs) that really got people talking. The ads were sponsored by drug education and prevention organizations such as The Partnership for a Drug-Free America (now called The Partnership at Drugfree.org). During one of the announcements, viewers saw butter sizzling in a hot pan on the stove. "This is drugs," said the narrator. An egg was cracked into

A popular PSA from the 1980s utilized a frying egg as a metaphor for a person's brain on drugs.

the pan and began to fry instantly. The narrator continued: "This is your brain on drugs. Any questions?"

No one expected drug-prevention PSAs to wipe out drug use in America. The goal was simply to get kids' attention. Young people had begun to see drugs as commonplace and safe. Yet statistics from hospitals, prisons, and scientific research labs told a radically different story. Drug educators wanted young people to realize that drugs are not risk-free.

So far, you've seen evidence to disprove Ecstasy's reputation as a harmless recreational drug. You know that Ecstasy alters the balance of natural chemicals in the body. This response may be so severe that users experience dangerously high body temperatures, dehydration,

or organ failure. You understand that Ecstasy may cause dependence. It can lead to the abuse of other drugs. And Ecstasy's impact reaches beyond the physical. Even casual use can affect your long-term goals. You may lose relationships, opportunities, or even be imprisoned.

Knowledge gives you the power to make choices. It forces you to think about your actions and allows you to help others. Share what you learn with friends and classmates. Talk to your parents and teachers, who may also be uninformed about this threat. Most importantly, set an example for younger siblings and neighbors. They look up to you and will follow your path.

Be in Touch

The Partnership at Drugfree.org provides an important reminder: Parents play an important role in preventing drug abuse. Kids say they appreciate this input, even if it's an awkward conversation. More than three-quarters of parents discuss the hazards of alcohol and marijuana abuse with their children. But only about 21 percent talk to their teens about Ecstasy. Why? In some cases, parents just don't know about this drug. Other parents think of Ecstasy as a rave drug. They might warn high

Having a conversation about drugs with a parent or guardian may sound difficult, but it is worth the time and effort.

school-aged teens about it, but assume it's not a problem among younger kids. Even the most conscientious parent has a hard time keeping up with issues in the teen community. That's where you can help.

Don't wait for a parent to begin the discussion about drug risks. Bring it up yourself. The effort really is worthwhile especially if you have younger siblings. The car is a good place to start awkward conversations. You don't have to sit face-to-face, and the ride gives you a few minutes of privacy. You can also write an e-mail or text a question. That gives your parents a little time to research answers and seek resources.

If the first effort is a success, schedule a family dinner to continue the conversation. You don't usually eat together? Give it a try! A study from Harvard Medical School looked at the benefits of family meals. It showed that children who eat with their families are less likely to use illegal drugs, cigarettes, or alcohol. These kids also ate healthier foods, and they tended to do better in school than those who ate alone. Your family doesn't have to make huge lifestyle changes to gain these benefits. Just eating a meal together a couple of times a week can bring your family closer, creating time to talk.

Be a Friend

You already know three important statistics about young people and Ecstasy:

- Youths generally don't think of Ecstasy as a risky drug.
- Adolescent use of Ecstasy has recently increased.
- Teens are less critical of their peers who use the drug.

These statistics tell us what people think about Ecstasy and how they use it. They don't describe the drug itself. If friends tell you that Ecstasy is harmless and everyone is using it, don't be afraid to set the story straight. Here are some good responses:

- Ecstasy is far from harmless. In fact, it's more dangerous now because of adulteration.
- Since 2002, annual Ecstasy use among eighth graders has remained near or below two percent. Put another way, 98 percent of eighth graders don't use it.
- Public opinion is not a good reason to use a drug. Health and safety come first.

Ask your closest friends what they have heard or experienced about Ecstasy and other drugs. Share what

56

you've learned, and make a plan in case uncomfortable situations arise. How will you respond if someone offers you Ecstasy? What can you do if peers give you a hard time for refusing to use it? When a friend has your back, it's a lot easier to be strong in the face of peer pressure.

While you are strengthening those relationships with family and friends, take time to get to know yourself. Teens often use drugs because they are bored. Ecstasy can cost $10 to $30 per dose. What useful things could you do with that money? Time is another gift. You can get a job, volunteer, or take up a sport; visit your grandparents, help a neighbor, or even write a book!

Life is full of challenges and changes, the embarrassment of mistakes, and the joy of successes. Ecstasy might temporarily make the lights brighter and the highs higher, but it doesn't provide you real happiness or love. Those gifts come from the relationships you build and the effort you put into the things you do every day.

Think back to that egg frying on the stove. You don't want that to represent you. This is life. This is your brain enjoying life. Any questions?

Glossary

adulterate to make less pure

adverse reaction any harmful side effect of a drug

anesthetic a drug that kills pain, often used during surgeries

cerebral cortex a part of the brain involved in functions including memory, learning, understanding language, thinking, and producing

dependence an emotional or physical need for a drug

drug a substance that changes how the body or brain functions

drug schedule the categories used to classify drugs, based on their potential for abuse and harm

ecstasy a feeling of overwhelming happiness; joy

empathy the ability to understand another's feelings or experiences

euphoria extreme happiness or joy

gateway drug a substance that leads users to abuse other, even more dangerous drugs

hallucination a sight, sound, or other sensation that is not real

hippocampus a part of the brain involved in memory and learning

hyperthermia unusually high body temperature that can be caused by the use of Ecstasy

hyponatremia a condition that occurs when there is not enough sodium (salt) in the body fluid; causes cells to swell dangerously

medicinal drug a drug used to treat or prevent disease

neurotoxin a substance that damages or destroys nerve cells

neurotransmitter chemicals that carry signals through the nervous system

overdose a large dose of a substance that causes a dangerous reaction in the body

paranoia unreasonable fear and suspicion

peer pressure words or actions from people of the same age group that suggest a person has to act or look the same to fit in

rave a party involving techno music and light shows

receptor a specific site on a nerve cell to which neurotransmitters can attach

recreational drug a chemical with no medical use, taken specifically to obtain a high

serotonin a neurotransmitter involved in the control of physical responses such as mood, alertness, and appetite

stimulant a class of drug taken to increase energy

synapse the microscopic space between two cells in the nervous system

synthesis production of chemicals in a laboratory

tolerance a reduction in the normal effects of a drug after regular use; requiring a larger dose to obtain the same effect

trafficking illegal sales of drugs

withdrawal symptoms that occur when a person who is physically dependent on a drug stops its use

Find Out More

Books

Bailey, Jacqui. *Taking Action Against Drugs*. New York:
Rosen Central, 2010.

LeVert, Suzanne with Jeff Hendricks. *Ecstasy.* New York:
Marshall Cavendish Benchmark, 2010.

Medina, Sarah. *Know the Facts About Drugs*. New York:
Rosen Central, 2010.

Rodger, Marguerite. *Party and Club Drugs.* New York:
Crabtree Publishing Company, 2012.

Websites

Above the Influence

http://www.abovetheinfluence.com/

> The National Youth Anti-Drug Media Campaign has
> worked in American communities since 1988, empow-
> ering young people to resist the influence of drugs.

Center for Substance Abuse Treatment (CSAT)

http://www.samhsa.gov/about/csat.aspx

> CSAT helps individuals and families find substance
> abuse treatment programs in their communities.
> Contact them at 240-276-1660.

Just Think Twice

http://www.justthinktwice.com/

Prepared especially for kids by the Drug Enforcement
Agency, this website provides information about a
variety of drugs commonly abused by teens and offers
links for those seeking support or treatment.

Nar-Anon and Nar-Ateen

http://www.nar-anon.org

These organizations offer support for the families
and friends of people addicted to drugs. Nar-Ateen
meetings are especially for young people ages 12 to 20.

The Science Behind Drug Abuse: Ecstasy

http://faculty.washington.edu/chudler/mdma.html

This website, also from the National Institute on Drug
Abuse, examines the effects of specific drugs on the
brain and body.

Index

Pages in **boldface** are illustrations.

About The Author

CHRISTINE PETERSEN has written more than fifty books for young people, covering a wide range of topics in science, health, and social studies. In her free time, Petersen enjoys hiking and snowshoeing with her son near their home in Minneapolis, Minnesota. She is a member of the Society of Children's Book Writers and Illustrators. She is a member of the Society of Children's Book Writers and Illustrators